AI and Mental Health
Transforming Therapy and Counseling

Table of Contents

Chapter 1. Introduction

As we navigate this era of astonishing digital transformation, our Special Report titled, "AI and Mental Health: Transforming Therapy and Counseling" acts as an essential beacon, spotlighting the intersection of cutting-edge Artificial Intelligence and the challenging landscape of mental health. Guided by the principle of simplicity, we unravel this deeply technical topic dexterously, presenting you with clear insights and digestible information, a venture that even those unaccustomed to technology can appreciate. Our report charts an enlightening course through the ways AI is reshaping our understanding of mental health and revolutionizing the delivery of therapy and counseling. It uncovers paths walked by scientists, therapists, and AI professionals in a bid to harness the immense potentials of AI for mental health. So why wait? Secure your copy today and embark on this journey of discovery that brilliantly bridges technology and mental well-being. Be part of the wave that's pioneering a new way forward, where technology and empathy are interwoven in the pursuit of mental health transformation.

Chapter 2. The Evolution of AI in Mental Health

The first known instance of machine-learning algorithms being applied to mental health data dates back to the 1960s. The rarefied air of cutting-edge research was filled with excitement as innovative thinkers started envisioning the myriad ways technology could be utilized for the betterment of our mental well-being. Let's delve into the archival records to trace the evolution of AI in mental health.

2.1. The Incipient Stage

The very foundation of AI in mental health can be traced back to Joseph Weizenbaum's creation in 1964 – ELIZA. Given the form of a natural language processing program, ELIZA gave the impression of understanding and responding to the user. The clinician Rogerian psychotherapist, 'Doctor' variant of this program, could carry out text-based dialogues, giving the illusion of empathy by reframing user's inputs into questions.

This archaic implementation of AI nudged the scientific community towards considering the possibility of digital solutions for mental health; albeit, ELIZA was severely restricted in its capacity. A lack of advanced technology meant the program had no real understanding of conversational context or human emotion, serving merely as an echo chamber.

2.2. Harnessing the Power of Machine Learning

The late 20th Century and early 21st Century witnessed an explosion of growth in the field of machine learning (ML). This period was vital in consolidating the place of AI in mental health care, as research and development focused on enhancing predictive capacities of AI systems, leading to advancements in psychiatry and psychology.

ML technologies began serving an instrumental role in analyzing complex mental health data, with an emphasis on predictive modeling. These models aided in the early detection of illnesses such as depression and anxiety and were trained on diverse data sets that ranged from written and spoken language to facial and emotional cues.

2.3. Emergence of AI-Powered Therapies

The emergence of AI-based CBT (Cognitive Behavioral Therapy) treatments during this period marked a significant breakthrough. These treatments leveraged the principles of machine learning to offer personalized therapy sessions. Research on AI-driven CBT has since grown exponentially, with a myriad of studies supporting its efficacy in conditions like Insomnia, Depression, and Anxiety.

Simultaneously, chatbots leveraging natural language processing algorithms began to feature prominently in digital mental health. Building on the simple structure of ELIZA, these chatbots now utilize machine learning algorithms to interpret human language better and provide personalized, real-time assistance.

2.4. Present-Day AI and Mental Health

Today, aided by advances in AI and digital technology, mental health care has reached unprecedented levels of accessibility and effectiveness. Deep Learning, a subset of machine learning, holds great promise in facilitating early detection and intervention for mental health disorders.

Multi-modal AI systems capable of extracting and analyzing information from disparate sources including - text, audio, and video, are transforming diagnosis and treatment. These algorithms can detect subtle patterns that may hint at a psychiatric condition, often before individuals can recognize these symptoms in themselves.

AI technologies have now stepped into the realm of psychiatry, with predictive modeling being used to strategize personalized treatment plans based on potentially foreseeable responses to different interventions.

Amid remarkable advances, several AI-driven mental health applications have been developed, enabling users to self-manage their mental health and access therapeutic support at their convenience. Notable examples include Woebot, a CBT-based chatbot developed to assist with symptoms of depression and anxiety, and Wysa, an 'emotionally intelligent' chatbot designed to improve mental resilience.

2.5. The Future: AI in Mental Health

The road from ELIZA to the present has been undeniably transformative. Looking forward, AI's potential in mental health care is virtually limitless. Advances in processing power, AI algorithms, and the increasing ubiquitousness of digital data will further fuel this evolution.

Parallelly, ethical considerations around AI in mental health are bound to become more complex and essential as the technology continues to evolve. Achieving a balance between harnessing AI's vast potential and adhering to stringent standards is the challenge that lies ahead.

This voyage through the annals of AI in mental health underscores the transformative nature of this intersection. As we continue to progress along this path, we may truly usher in a new era where mental health care is widely accessible, preventative, personalized, and, perhaps most importantly, highly effective. The evolution that we have traced here is, indeed, just the beginning of this enthrallingly promising journey.

Chapter 3. Understanding Mental Health: A Brief Overview

Understanding mental health is a crucial first step in appreciating the transformative potential of AI in the domain of therapy and counseling. Long regarded as a nebulous and often taboo subject, mental health occupies an increasingly central role in our understanding of overall health and well-being.

3.1. The Concept of Mental Health

Mental health can be referred to as an amalgam of our emotional, psychological, and social well-being. It is not just the absence of mental illness. Instead, it envelops the complete spectrum of thoughts, feelings, and behaviors that impact our ability to cope with life's stresses, work productively, contribute meaningfully to our communities, and realize our abilities.

Mental health changes over time, influenced by a myriad of factors including physiological changes, environmental stressors, and psychological factors. The concept of mental health is broad and includes aspects of life satisfaction, perceived self-efficacy, autonomy, competence, reliance on others, and recognition of the ability to realize one's intellectual and emotional potential.

3.2. Mental Health Disorders

Mental disorders, also referred to as mental illnesses, are health conditions that involve changes in thinking, emotions, or behavior, or a combination of these. They are associated with distress and problems functioning in social, work, or family situations. Common mental disorders include depression, anxiety, bipolar affective disorder, schizophrenia, and other psychoses.

According to the World Health Organization (WHO), around 970 Million people worldwide suffer from mental health or substance use disorders. Depression and anxiety are the most common mental disorders, with more than 300 million people affected by depression, and a further 260 million living with anxiety disorders.

3.3. Biological Aspect of Mental Health

A large body of research indicates that mental health disorders are often tied to biological factors. Mental illnesses are brain-based conditions that affect thinking, emotions, and behaviors. Scientists believe many mental illnesses are linked to abnormalities in many genes, not just one. That is why a person inherits a susceptibility to a mental disorder and doesn't necessarily develop the illness.

Stress and factors such as genetic vulnerability can disrupt brain functioning and lead to various mental illnesses. The most prominent biological theory about mental illness is the neurotransmitter theory. Neurotransmitters are chemical substances that allow information to flow from one nerve cell to another. Dysfunctions in these neurotransmitters can contribute to mental health disorders.

3.4. Environmental Factors and Mental Health

Environment plays a critical role in shaping an individual's mental health. Environmental factors like a traumatic personal history, family history of mental health issues, long-term physical health conditions, and experiencing discrimination or stigma can all contribute to mental health problems.

Factors such as a dysfunctional family setup, marriage or relationship problems, financial difficulties, loneliness and isolation are also strongly associated with poorer mental health outcomes. It's such a wide range of factors that emphasizes the necessity of a holistic approach to mental health.

3.5. The Stigma of Mental Health

Despite understanding and awareness of mental health being on the rise, mental illness continues to carry a significant stigma. People with mental health problems often describe feeling isolated, ostracized, and shamed. Many a time, this stigma is rooted in misconceptions and prejudices, resulting in a general lack of understanding and empathy towards those suffering from mental health conditions.

For a robust mental health system, it is essential to eliminate the stigma associated with mental health conditions. Efforts should be directed towards sensitizing individuals about mental health, encouraging supportive behavior, and promoting acceptance and inclusivity.

3.6. The Evolution of Mental Health Treatment

Mental health treatment has seen significant changes throughout history. Ancient civilizations suspected supernatural causes behind mental disorders, while the Middle Ages deemed them a product of witchcraft. Early attempts to treat mental health conditions were often cruel and unscientific. The 18th and 19th centuries marked a mental health movement with the establishment of asylums. However, the conditions were typically abysmal, with patients often suffering brutal and degrading treatment.

The advent of psychotherapy in the early 20th century marked a significant shift in the understanding and treatment of mental health disorders. It enabled a near-universal understanding that mental health conditions are legitimate illnesses deserving specialized, compassionate treatment.

In more recent times, there has been a shift towards community-based care and a push for deinstitutionalization. Medications have also improved considerably and serve as viable treatment options for many mental health conditions.

Despite these advancements, a substantial treatment gap remains, with many individuals who need help not being able to access the required services. These challenges have opened up new horizons for the application of technology in mental health, with AI playing a transformative role. As we move forward into the deeper sections of this report, we delve into the possibilities that AI offers in bridging this treatment gap and accelerating mental health innovation.

Chapter 4. Deciphering AI: Bridging the Technical Gap

Artificial Intelligence (AI), a term once relegated to science fiction, has become a hallmark of our daily lives. Within the expanding sphere of AI's applications, its potential for transforming the mental health landscape is emerging as a topic of crucial importance. However, this convergence of AI and mental health engagement can be complex to understand. Let's start by demystifying AI, its components, and how it allows us to interpret and react to mental health concerns more effectively.

4.1. What is Artificial Intelligence?

Artificial Intelligence refers to the simulation of human intelligence processes by machines. These processes mainly include learning, reasoning, self-correction, and the ability to perform tasks that require human intelligence, such as understanding natural language, recognizing patterns, problem-solving, and intuitive decision-making.

AI operates based on algorithms or set rules that guide its function. These algorithms can be simple, only using specified inputs to produce predictable outputs or more complex models that simulate neural networks enabling machine learning. Importantly, AI isn't just about mimicking human brains. It's also about surpassing human limitations, by processing vast amounts of data quickly and accurately.

4.2. Behind the AI Curtain: Machine Learning

A key facet of AI is Machine Learning (ML), a process where AI systems learn from data, identify patterns, and make decisions with minimal human intervention. ML is made possible by more complex algorithms that improve their operations "intelligently" over time. Consider an AI system designed to detect anxiety. By training on a vast dataset of different interactions, the system can learn the correlation between particular behavioral attributes and anxiety, further fine-tuning its detection abilities with every interaction.

4.3. Deep Learning: Simulating Human Brains

Deep Learning, a subtype of ML, draws inspiration directly from the human brain. It employs artificial neural networks (ANN) which structurally echo human neurons. Deep Learning models can delve into multilevel interpretation, understanding the context at different layers, much like our cognitive processes. The potential applications in mental health are exciting — recognizing subtle vocal fluctuations indicating stress, for instance.

4.4. Innovation at the Intersection: Natural Language Processing

Another pivotal revolution in AI that serves mental health is Natural Language Processing (NLP). NLP helps machines understand, interpret, and generate human language—a previously insurmountable challenge. NLP, by enabling human-computer interaction, can be effectively used in digital mental health interviews, wherein conversation is key. An AI with NLP could understand patient speech, recognize emotion, and respond empathetically, bypassing boundaries of human therapists' availability.

4.5. AI Ethics and Transparency: The Key to Trust

Although AI-based technologies can substantially augment mental health interventions, it's crucial to maintain transparency and ethical practices. AI functioning should be interpretable by non-tech users—such as therapists—enhancing trust in technology. Additionally, designing AI should involve a wide range of stakeholders, including mental health professionals, patients, and ethicists, to ensure inclusivity and responsible data use.

Understanding the technological mechanics of AI—their complexities and possibilities—can empower us to leverage this incredible tool for mental health transformation. With knowledge comes power, and our comprehension of AI can bridge the technical gap, opening doors to practical applications in therapy and counseling. This comprehension ensures that the union of AI and mental health isn't just about technology, but foremost about empathy and understanding, reinforcing our collective pursuit of mental health improvement.

Chapter 5. AI Applications in Mental Health: A Global Outlook

Understanding the global expanse of Artificial Intelligence in mental health asks that we consider its manifold applications and implications, diving deep into the breadth and depth of this promising collaboration.

5.1. The Emergence of AI in Mental Health

Artificial Intelligence, in the world of mental health, emerged as a game-changer the same way it did in other fields - with significant promise of revolutionizing the sector from the ground up. To truly appreciate this shift, we need to travel back to the infancy of AI. It all started with ELIZA, our first attempt at creating a chatbot psychotherapist in the 1960s, paving the path for future dialogues around AI and mental health.

In the past decade, we are witnessing an unprecedented acceleration of this interplay. The convergence of AI with cognitive psychology and neuroscience has given rise to promising avenues for understanding, diagnosing, and treating mental health issues; a transformation birthed from our collective craving for optimized, personalized care.

5.2. AI for Mental Health Diagnosis

Diagnosing mental illnesses often involve nuanced, subjective analysis of a patient's feelings, behaviors, and thoughts over time.

The traditional process, while effective, faces limitations in terms of scalability, efficiency and subjectivity. Enter AI, equipped with advanced machine learning algorithms. These tools plunge into numerous psychological, sociological, and physical parameters, offering a more holistic, objective diagnoses.

Take the example of Mindstrong Health, a digital platform that employs machine learning to assess digital biomarkers. It provides vital information about a patient's mood, cognition, and behavior by analyzing passively collected data on smartphone use. Predictive models thus generated aid in early identification and intervention of mental health disorders.

5.3. AI-Powered Therapeutic Interventions

But AI's role does not stop with identification alone. It extends into the provision of therapeutic interventions as well. AI-based smart applications today facilitate Cognitive Behavioral Therapy (CBT), Dialectical Behavioral Therapy (DBT), and Mindfulness-Based Cognitive Therapy (MBCT) among others.

Consider Woebot, an automated conversational agent delivering CBT for depression and anxiety. Research shows engagement with Woebot results in significant reductions in symptoms of depression relative to a control group. Likewise, Tess by X2AI, offers psychological therapy through text messages, its algorithms adapting to the specific needs and responses of the individual user.

5.4. AI Tracking Mental Health Trends Across Populations

Through a detailed analysis of the data available on social platforms, AI tools can identify trends in mental health and detect early indications of a potential mental health crisis. For instance, machine learning algorithms have helped researchers understand the manifestation of depression in language patterns and social media interactions.

Software like Qntfy's 'OurDataHelps' collects data from users' digital presence to predict mental health crises. Such initiatives provide insights into a population's mental health, empowering intervention at a larger scale and forming a part of public health strategy.

5.5. Global Acceptance and Implementation

China is a leader in adopting AI for mental health support. Chinese app, Know Yourself, developed by Ali Health uses AI technology to provide psychiatric services, serving as a powerful tool in a country where the ratio of psychiatrists to the population is highly skewed. In the US, Quartet Health is making strides in AI-facilitated collaborative care. Their platform uses AI to identify patients with hidden mental health conditions and connects them with appropriate care.

The emerging economies aren't lagging either. India's pioneer AI startup, Wysa, designed an AI chatbot, assisting millions worldwide in managing stress, anxiety, and sleep issues, through an empathetic, anonymous conversation.

AI is transforming mental health treatment across the globe, with developers creatively adapting technology to suit distinct societal and cultural needs. However, for all its promise, the integration of AI in mental health also introduces valid ethical and professional considerations.

5.6. Ethical Implications

The application of AI in mental health sparks debates surrounding confidentiality, privacy, accuracy, accountability, cultural competency, and more. Stringent guidelines to address these concerns, balancing the integrity of AI applications while respecting patients' rights, are crucial moving forward.

AI in mental health brings forth a new reality - one where technology assists human effort in understanding our innermost complexities, navigating our path towards a mentally healthy globe. The journey has just begun, but the possibilities teeter on the edge of tomorrow. Today, we stand on an important precipice, bearing witness to the dawn of a transformation that envisions a seamlessly integrated landscape of AI and mental health. Dare we take the leap? Only time will tell. Yet, the promise is immense and undeniable. The age of AI in mental health is just beginning, and it's an exciting groundbreaking journey we're on.

Chapter 6. Transforming Therapy: Unveiling AI-powered Solutions

It's no longer a prediction but a reality – Artificial Intelligence is drastically reshaping numerous sectors including healthcare, with an intense focus on mental health. Its applications span from forecasting possible mental health issues to providing digital therapy, a novel trend that is gaining considerable momentum worldwide.

6.1. AI's Approach Towards Mental Health: An Overview

The integration of AI in mental health services is driven by the rising prevalence of mental health disorders, the unfortunate stigma attached to mental health, and the dire shortage of mental health professionals, especially in remote or underprivileged areas. These could potentially be met with an AI-powered platform able to provide timely and accessible mental healthcare to those who need it regardless of geographical location.

AI has been successful in the early detection of mental health issues by analyzing a vast array of clues: changes in voice tonality, facial expressions, choice of words, and even keyboard stroke patterns. With such criteria, algorithms are trained to identify patterns proving useful to clinicians and researchers in the diagnosis and monitoring of mental health disorders such as depression, anxiety, and PTSD.

6.2. AI-based Therapy Tools

There is a gamut of AI-based tools making significant strides in therapy and counseling. Chatbots, for instance, use natural language processing to simulate human-like interactions providing users with a safe space for meaningful self-disclosure. They are designed to provide immediate responses, unconditional support, and psychological intervention whenever required.

Apps like Woebot, Wysa, and Youper leverage AI and Cognitive Behavioral Therapy (CBT) principles to help users monitor their emotions, understand their mood patterns, and learn healthy coping strategies. These tools are accessible 24/7, thereby providing continuous support, which is far from possible with traditional face-to-face sessions.

6.3. AI-guided Predictive Analyses and Therapy Personalization

AI-powered algorithms are proficient at detecting patterns and predicting outcomes. In the context of mental health, AI can analyze a variety of data like genetic information, medical history, and even online activity to draw connections between these factors and the risk of developing certain mental health disorders.

Such predictive analytics can provide early warning signs for people at risk of mental health problems, allowing preemptive steps to be taken. At the same time, these insights are crucial for personalizing treatment plans. Every individual responds differently to therapies, and AI can help stratify patients based on their likely responses to different treatments, thereby ensuring the efficient use of healthcare resources.

6.4. The Role of Virtual Reality in AI-powered Therapy

Virtual Reality (VR) is another AI application rapidly transforming psychopathology treatment. VR therapy, or "VRET," places patients in a computer-generated world. By provoking stimuli within a controlled environment, therapists can gradually expose patients to their fears and teach them effective coping strategies. This approach has shown significant potential in the treatment of disorders such as PTSD, phobias, and social anxiety.

6.5. Ethical Considerations and the Path Forward

AI's role within mental health treatment continues to emerge, but it's not without debate. Privacy of data, data accuracy, and the potential for machines to fully comprehend human emotion are areas of contention. However, AI isn't intended to replace human therapists, but rather to augment their capabilities by providing immediate, prompt, and personalized care.

We cannot overlook the considerable advantages AI provides in mental health treatment. With ongoing development, we will see more refined algorithms, more intuitive AI therapists, and more personalized treatment plans, always prioritizing the well-being of individuals. While AI does not have all the answers to our mental health crises, it is an ally as we move toward uncharted therapeutic territories.

Chapter 7. AI and Counseling: A New Era of Support

Mental health, a field traditionally dominated by human interactions and empathy, is now seeing the transformative influence of Artificial Intelligence (AI). As we stand on the brink of this new era, the coupling of AI with counseling gives birth to a new paradigm of therapy - one that promises increased accessibility, affordability, and personalization. However, before we dive deeper into the role of AI in counseling, it's important that we understand the mechanistics of AI itself.

7.1. Understanding AI: From Logic to Learning

AI, at its core, is the simulation of human intelligence processes by machines. These processes include learning (the acquisition of information and rules), reasoning (using rules to reach approximate or definite conclusions), and self-correction.

AI operates on the principle of receiving inputs and using programmed logic to generate an output. This logic was initially hardcoded, contingent on specific responses. However, the staggering volume and complexity of human behaviors, emotions, and mental patterns soon made this approach obsolete.

Enter Machine Learning - the idea that systems can learn from data, identify patterns, and make decisions. Rather than rely on explicit programming, machine learning uses statistical and probabilistic approaches to understand underlying features and structures within the data, building predictive models. And further evolving from Machine Learning, we witness the potential of Deep Learning, where high-level abstractions and data representations can be used through a composition of multiple nonlinear transformations.

7.2. AI in Counseling: A Prospect of Paradigm Shift

AI offers several ways to augment counseling practices. Driven by nuances of data, AI can illuminate hidden patterns in mental health, helping counselors develop more effective treatment plans. Furthermore, AI-powered applications and chatbots are now in service, allowing clients to seek help anytime, anywhere.

Chatbots in counseling, often called 'therapy bots,' are designed to communicate with users in a manner that replicates human conversation. They offer support by providing instant mental health tools, psychoeducation, and coping strategy recommendations.

These bots aren't devised to replace human therapists entirely; rather, they bridge gaps in mental healthcare by being accessible around the clock. Therapy bots can ease the burden of routine check-ins and symptom tracking, allowing human therapists to focus on higher-level therapeutic tasks.

7.3. Capturing Signals: Sensors and Wearable Technology

In terms of physiological responses and emotional cues, the human body is a trove of information. AI is leveraged to capture, interpret, and utilize this information using sensors and wearable technology. Devices such as smartwatches, wristbands, and applications on smartphones can monitor heart rate, stress levels, sleep patterns, and physical activity.

By analyzing the data collected, these devices can be used to assess an individual's mental health status. Changes or patterns in the data can provide visual signals of stress or an impending mental health crisis, allowing timely intervention and support.

7.4. AI In Teletherapy: Erasing Borders

Teletherapy, another avenue where AI has made significant strides, is the provision of therapy through a digital platform. In today's interconnected world where geographical boundaries no longer define access to mental healthcare, AI is immensely useful in managing online appointments, reminders, tracking progress, and offering a streamlined online therapy experience.

AI-powered platforms can analyze voice and text inputs from therapy sessions and provide therapists with insights about mood states, speech patterns, and potential risk factors.

7.5. Ethics and Concerns: The Conflux of Technology and Humanity

As remarkable as the symbiosis between AI and counseling may be, it also raises crucial ethical questions. The overarching concern revolves around data privacy and security. Therapeutic communications necessitate utmost confidentiality. Therefore, determining who can access the data, how it's stored, and its security become critical considerations in ethical AI use.

Concerns also arise around the impersonality of AI in therapy. Despite advancements, AI cannot yet fully replicate human empathy and warmth. The professional judgment of a human therapist remains the cornerstone in the field of mental health.

Navigating these ethical dilemmas may be challenging, but it also primes us to tread a path where we coincide technology with the tenderness of human connection, leading towards a mental health landscape reshaped by the revolutionary benefits of AI while being mindful of its limitations.

In conclusion, the integration of AI in counseling presents opportunities for enhanced mental health support in a digitalizing world. By facilitating better understanding, increasing accessibility, and assisting in early detection and intervention, AI is changing the face of counseling as we know it. However, on this path of digital transformation, it is critical to remember that true mental healthcare is patient-centric, empathetic, and above all, rooted in the principles of humanistic counseling.

Chapter 8. Case Studies: Success Stories of AI in Mental Health

Over the past few years, multiple AI-driven projects, each with unique goals, insights, and outcomes, have successfully been implemented in the arena of mental health. This chapter aims to savor these innovative and impactful initiatives, shedding light on how they have each contributed significantly to the understanding, diagnosis, and treatment of mental health conditions.

8.1. Woebot: AI-Powered CBT

One of the most publicized AI interventions in mental health in recent years is the conversational agent, Woebot. Developed by a team of Stanford psychologists and AI experts, Woebot utilizes AI and natural language processing (NLP) to administer cognitive-behavioral therapy (CBT) through daily, personalized, and interactive conversations with users on Facebook Messenger.

Woebot covers topics like thought distortions, mindfulness, and mood tracking. In a study conducted over a two-week period, users who interacted daily with Woebot reported significant reductions in depression symptoms compared to a control group.

The success of Woebot lies in its accessibility - therapy at one's convenience, removing barriers like cost, stigma, and geographical location. It also points to the powerful potential for AI to democratize mental health resources.

8.2. Tess: An AI Mental Health Chatbot

Another AI innovation making waves in mental health is Tess by X2 AI. Through its intelligent, emotional analytics and psychological artificial intelligence, Tess provides psychological support, follows up with patients, and offers self-help strategies to cope with stress or anxiety. By learning each interaction's context, Tess engages in empathetic conversations, taking mental health intervention to another level.

Clinical trials involving Tess showed impressive results. In a study involving college students, those who interacted with Tess reported a significant decrease in symptoms of depression and anxiety over two weeks. Tess' unique advantage is being available 24/7, providing help to those who might not ordinarily be able to access professional support.

8.3. Ellipsis Health: Machine Learning for Depression Detection

Ellipsis Health has developed a machine learning algorithm that analyzes human speech to detect signs of depression and anxiety. Through this method, Ellipsis Health aims to streamline the diagnostic process and make mental health treatment more accessible.

Their technology has been proven in multiple clinical trials to distinguish between healthy individuals and those with depression or anxiety. The application of this technology can play a pivotal role in the early identification and treatment of mental health disorders.

8.4. Praava Health: Analytics-Based Mental Health Diagnosis

Praava Health uses AI technology to develop a mood and sentiment analyzer to evaluate conversations in the mental health space. Their innovation is designed to analyze and categorize speech into different mood profiles, aiding the diagnostic process.

Patients' experiences during clinical trials of Praava Health's model suggest that it is useful for both diagnosing and tracking mental health issues over time. The success of Praava Health's AI algorithm emphasizes the potential for integrating AI in mental health diagnostics, as it enables a rapid analysis of symptoms and quick identification of mood disorders.

8.5. Zia: AI-Enhanced Therapy Sessions

Zia is a voice-enabled AI tool located in the therapy room to help therapists better capture their clients' thoughts, feelings, and behaviors. By analyzing therapy sessions in real time, Zia helps mental health professionals make informed decisions about treatment.

Using AI, it can easily detect patterns and trends in clients' speech and behavior that might be missed by a human therapist. It captures nuanced alterations in the client's tone, mood, and linguistic patterns, which may indicate emerging mental health concerns.

A pilot initiative with Zia indicated clinicians found it valuable and convenient, due to a reduction in manual note-taking, improved documentation, and insights derived from objective pattern identification.

In conclusion, these AI implementations in mental health exhibit how technology can be harnessed to improve access, enhance diagnosis and treatment, and make therapy more impactful. The stories of Woebot, Tess, Ellipsis Health, Praava Health, and Zia represent just a snapshot of the current AI advancements redefining mental health landscape. As technology evolves, the conviction grows stronger: AI promises a future with better mental health care for everyone.

Chapter 9. Ethical Implications and Concerns in AI-driven Therapy

Given the spectacular advancements of AI in the domain of mental health, it is essential to appraise its ethical dimensions. By dissecting and addressing a miscellany of ethical concerns, this report intends to stimulate ethical discussions around AI's therapeutic applications.

9.1. Data Security and Privacy

A paramount concern in AI-driven therapy pertains to data security and privacy. The AI therapy model operates with the elementary requirement of data – a comprehensive encapsulation of patient history, emotional states, and other personal specifics. Given the sensitivity of this information, it is susceptible to breaches and misuse, raising doubts about its confidentiality. Studies reveal a reasonable apprehension among patients about data security in digital therapeutic ventures, reinforcing the necessity to devise durable safeguards.

Moreover, various legal frameworks and data handling guidelines, such as the General Data Protection Regulation (GDPR) in the European Union and the Health Insurance Portability and Accountability Act (HIPAA) in the United States, necessitate concrete strategies to ensure patients' privacy rights. Such legislation impose liabilities not just on the providers of mental healthcare but also on the AI developers and third-party contractors they work with.

9.2. AI Bias and Misdiagnosis

Another prevalent ethical dilemma arises due to the potential bias and misdiagnosis that AI models might present. A common critique of AI is its propensity to reflect the biases of its design, data collection, or training. These flaws might result in skewed recommendations that could ultimately lead to a misdiagnosis. In the realm of mental health, this could be particularly devastating as the repercussions could further escalate the patients' emotional distress and may even lead to self-harm or suicide.

For instance, if an AI model is trained predominantly on data from a specific demographic, it might not perform adequately when presented with data from other diverse groups. This could not only lead to disparity in treatment efficacy, but it could also perpetuate systemic biases present in healthcare delivery, thereby alienating certain groups or minorities.

9.3. Inadequate Human Interaction

While AI-driven therapy creates accessibility and allows anonymity, it can potentially result in a lack of human interaction, an integral aspect of traditional therapy. In traditional mental health therapy, professionals rely on non-verbal cues to understand a patient's emotional condition, something that an AI system inherently lacks. Additionally, AI models, at their current state, would likely fail to emulate the empathetic human touch, leaving patients feeling unheard or misunderstood.

9.4. Algorithm Transparency

Algorithmic transparency is another contentious issue in AI-driven therapy. The concepts of AI and machine learning are difficult for non-technical people to understand due to their complexity. A lack of understanding can cause patients to develop misconceptions or unwarranted fear towards these technologies, potentially deterring them from seeking help. Similarly, healthcare providers might feel apprehensive about adopting these tools if they are unsure of the algorithm's decision-making process.

However, in many circumstances, even the creators of the AI models aren't entirely sure how their algorithms make certain decisions. This absence of clear explanation is often referred to as the 'black box' problem. When it comes to mental health, this opacity can have severe consequences, especially when AI's recommendation diverges from conventional treatment methods, leading to uncertainty and skepticism.

9.5. Autonomy and Consent

Equally paramount is the consideration of patient autonomy and consent. To engage patients in AI-based therapy, it's essential to solicit informed consent, considering they comprehend the technology, its potential benefits, and risks. However, providing such detailed understanding can be arduous, given the complexity of AI. Yet, it is crucial - offering AI-driven therapy without informed consent could gravely affect patients' autonomy.

9.6. conclusion

In sum, while AI's transformative potential in mental healthcare is vast, it brings along a host of ethical challenges. Recognizing these issues will be crucial in ensuring the harmony of technology and therapy. It's encouraging to note, however, that discussions around these concerns are gaining momentum among researchers, practitioners, and policymakers, marking the first step towards curing these ethical dilemmas.

Chapter 10. The Future of AI in Mental Health: Predictions and Possibilities

As the tendrils of Artificial Intelligence (AI) advance deeper into the realm of mental health, they begin to entwine in intricate patterns, forming a new landscape peppered with unprecedented possibilities. Unmoored from the traditional frameworks of therapy and counseling, AI emerges as a beacon of innovation and change, driving mental health towards a future brimming with untold prospects.

10.1. The Dawn of AI-Powered Diagnosis

Sifting through the complex layers of human behavior, uncovering tangled webs of emotions, and connecting the dots to form a comprehensive diagnosis is a task that challenges even the most skilled therapists. This painstaking dance can often be time-consuming, expensive, and sometimes, less than perfect. Enter AI, equipped with sophisticated machine learning algorithms that can process vast amounts of data to identify patterns and trends beyond human cognitive capabilities.

Whether it's deciphering subtle changes in speech patterns or interpreting changes in mood via biometric analysis, AI has shown promise in diagnosing mental health conditions with remarkable accuracy. It provides a more objective basis for diagnosis, reducing the likelihood of subjectivity present in human-to-human assessments. Importantly, its capabilities extend to recognizing early signs of disorders, prompting intervention before conditions escalate.

10.2. AI: A Resilient Ally in Teletherapy

Covid-19 catapulted teletherapy to the forefront, an unexpected consequence of the global crisis that has now become a lifeline for many patients grappling with mental health issues. AI plays a vital role in this context. Through chatbots, AI can deliver Cognitive Behavioral Therapy (CBT) to patients from the comfort of their homes, removing geographical and social barriers.

These "Virtual Therapists" aren't confined to a 40-minute session schedule. They provide round-the-clock support, and use real-time data to adapt therapy sessions specific to the user's responses. This could revolutionize accessibility of mental health resources, particularly beneficial in regions where mental healthcare provision is inadequate.

10.3. Improving Mental Health Treatments with AI

At present, choosing the right treatment often involves a trial-and-error method. AI strengthens the therapy toolbox by personalizing treatments based on detailed analysis of individual patterns and responses. It can help predict which medication might be more effective for a particular individual, or even determine if psychotherapy would be a better choice.

Precision in treatment selection means avoiding the pitfalls of ineffective therapies and bypassing the toll they take on a patient's wellbeing. It also holds the potential to reduce the burden on healthcare systems, limiting the number of clinical visits and allocating resources more judiciously.

10.4. AI Enhancing Preventive Measures

The concept of preventive mental health embodies the phrase, 'prevention is better than cure.' Here, AI, with its ability to analyze copious amounts of data swiftly and accurately, excels at identifying potential risk factors for mental health disorders. By processing a range of variables such as genetic predispositions, lifestyle choices, environmental factors, and even social media behavior, AI can provide vital insights for mental health prevention strategies.

Employing these predictions, preventive initiatives can be individualized, helping individuals avoid negative mental health outcomes. If broadly implemented, it could dramatically reduce the global burden of mental illnesses.

10.5. Ethics and Data Privacy Concerns

While the horizon of AI benefits in mental health appears promising, it throws a cautionary shadow over the critical issue of data privacy. Since AI systems thrive on data, these concerns are essential. There is an implicit responsibility to ensure sensitive mental health data is protected, maintaining the trust of those who share it.

Regulations ensuring ethical use of AI, and stringent data privacy policies should be standardized across the globe, ensuring the sustained adoption and support of AI in mental health. These measures can prevent potential misuse of information, and ensure patient dignity and confidentiality remain sacrosanct.

In conclusion, AI holds great promise for the future of mental health. By shaping diagnosis, treatment, prevention, and interventions, it's poised to influence every facet of mental health care. However, in the rush to adopt and implement AI, it's paramount that ethics and data protection remain at the core, safeguarding the integrity of mental healthcare. While we might not be able to predict the future with certainty, one thing remains clear: The potential of AI in mental health is tremendous, and offers a hopeful vision of what the future might hold.

Chapter 11. How To Advocate for AI Integration in Mental Health Services

Artificial Intelligence (AI) has been steadily reshaping numerous fields, promising greater accuracy, efficiency, and scope. One such beneficiary is the mental health sector, where successful incorporation of AI can improve the quality, accessibility, and customization of services. Advocating for AI integration in mental health services necessitates stakeholder awareness, regulatory readiness, appropriate funding, and environment preparation. Herein, we explore these aspects.

11.1. Understanding the Capabilities of AI

The first step towards effectively advocating for AI integration in mental health services entails being well-versed in its capabilities and specific applications. AI, including machine learning, deep learning, and natural language processing, can analyze large amounts of data and identify patterns often missed by humans. AI's capabilities extend to analyzing language and speech patterns to detect signs of mental health issues, powering chatbots that deliver cognitive behavioral therapy (CBT), and predicting relapses based on social media behavior. Ensuring stakeholders appreciate this transformative potential is fundamental to building momentum for integration.

11.2. Highlighting the Benefits

The benefits of AI integration into mental health services are numerous. They include increased access to care—particularly in remote and underserved communities, 24x7 availability, reduced stigma associated with seeking therapy, personalized treatment plans, and implementation of predictive strategies for preventive care. AI can also ease the workload for therapists, allowing them to focus their energy and expertise on more complex cases. Sharing case studies and tangible success stories can make a compelling argument and helps illuminate the direct advantages of AI integration.

11.3. Addressing Ethical Concerns and Privacy

Addressing ethical concerns and privacy issues must be at the forefront of any advocacy efforts. AI's applications in mental health need to be developed and used in a way that respects individual rights and ensures confidentiality. Transparency is crucial in AI-driven therapy, and patients should fully understand how AI is involved in their treatment. Concerns on bias in data sets and AI systems should be tackled head-on, with robust protocols to ensure unbiased, equitable services.

11.4. Encouraging Collaboration

An often-overlooked aspect of advocacy involves promoting collaboration between tech companies, AI developers, social workers, therapists, and patients. Creating a dialogue between these groups can ensure that AI tools are thoughtfully designed, ethically applied, and genuinely beneficial. Advocacy should thus include the promotion of forums and workshops that encourage interactions and knowledge exchange among these stakeholders.

11.5. Preparing the Regulatory Environment

Regulatory readiness is critical for the successful integration of AI in mental health services. The cross-section of health and digital technology necessitates specific regulations to ensure safety, privacy, and efficacy. Advocates must lobby for advancements in policy to match the pace of technological development.

11.6. Funding

Funding is a crucial component for AI integration, and advocates need to work on gaining financial backing. This involves collecting empirical evidence that quantifies AI's impact in terms of cost-efficiency and positive health outcomes to present a compelling case to potential investors or government bodies.

11.7. Preparing the Environment

Finally, patient and professional acceptance is key. It requires creating an environment of trust and acceptance, as resistance to change can pose a significant barrier to AI integration. Focus on preparing medical personnel for this transition, involving them in the development of AI solutions, and providing adequate training on the use of AI tools. Patients, too, should be educated about AI-driven tools and their advantages.

To sum up, advocating for AI integration in mental health services involves a keen understanding of AI's capabilities, highlighting its potential benefits, addressing ethical concerns, developing robust, relevant regulations, securing funding, and nurturing an environment receptive to change. Taking a proactive, inclusive, and collaborative approach towards advocacy will go a long way in ensuring successful AI integration in mental health services, opening doors for improved patient care and outcomes.